Subpoena Compliance,
Appearance, Objection,
and
Protective Orders
in
Arizona Mental Health Practice

Subpoena Compliance, Appearance, Objection, and Protective Orders in Arizona Mental Health Practice

Scott David Stewart, Esq.
and
Robert C. Howard, Jr., Esq.

An Imprint of Stewart Law Group
www.ArizonaLawGroup.com

Published in 2016 by Stewart Law Group USA

• 777 E Thomas Rd Ste 210, Phoenix AZ 85014 •
• 1490 S Price Rd Ste 212, Chandler AZ 85286 •
• 17470 N Pacesetter Way, Scottsdale AZ 85255 •
• 14050 N 83rd Ave Ste 290, Peoria AZ 85381 •
• 1910 S Stapley Dr Ste 221, Mesa AZ 85204 •
• 20325 N 51st Ave Ste 134, Glendale AZ 85308 •

www.arizonalawgroup.com

FIRST EDITION

ISBN 978-0-9886052-6-8

For information please write:

Stewart Law Group
777 E Thomas Rd Ste 210
Phoenix AZ 85014

Legal Disclaimer

The general information in this book is not, nor is it intended to be, specific legal advice. You should consult an attorney for specific legal advice regarding your individual situation.

This book is provided as a general reference work and is for informational purposes only. You are advised to check for changes to current law and to consult with a qualified attorney on any legal issue. The receipt of or use of this book does not create an attorney-client relationship with Stewart Law Group or any of its attorneys.

This book is provided as a general reference work and is for informational purposes only. Because this book was prepared for a general readership, without investigation into the facts of each particular case, it is not legal advice. Neither Stewart Law Group nor any of its attorneys has an attorney-client relationship with you. The thoughts and commentary about the law contained in this book are provided merely as a public service and do not constitute solicitation or legal advice.

While we endeavored to provide accurate information in this book, we cannot guarantee that the material provided herein is accurate, adequate, or complete. This general legal information is provided on an 'as is' basis. We make no warranties and disclaim liability for damages resulting from its use. Legal advice must be tailored to the specific circumstances of each case and laws are constantly changing, so nothing provided in this book should be used as a substitute for the advice of competent counsel. The material in this book may be considered advertising under applicable rules.

Contents

I

Introduction

At some point in your capacity as an Arizona mental health professional, you, a colleague, or an associate will be served with a subpoena for information about a patient.

In that situation, psychiatrists, psychologists, therapists, licensed social workers, and counselors alike need instructive reference materials at their fingertips. Subpoenas seldom allow the luxury of time to contemplate next moves. Adding to the professional's already overflowing schedule, there is no time to waste and little time for deliberation.

After reading through this book on *Subpoena Compliance, Appearance, Objection, and Protective Orders in Arizona Mental Health Practice*, file it away for that rainy day which, like all stormy weather, is inevitable. Although this book is not legal advice, the information provided herein is current through the end of 2015. Laws do change. Judges can and do interpret laws differently. Therefore, always seek competent legal advice about your specific situation.

2

Why Family Lawyers Subpoena Mental Health Professionals

There are several discovery tools used by Arizona attorneys to help unearth information relevant to the case – namely subpoenas, releases, interrogatories, depositions, requests for admission, and requests for production of documents.

First, a subpoena is an order served on the custodian of certain records and information pertaining to a lawsuit. Second, the subpoena is widely used to gather patient information that could be admissible as evidence in a court proceeding or trial. Third, any evidence gathering by subpoena, or some other discovery device, may lead to further requests for additional information and testimony.

Stepping back for just a moment, recognizing why family lawyers seek mental health information to bolster their clients' cases can be helpful.

3

Legal Strategy in Family Law Cases

As a subpoenaed person, the psychotherapist or counselor should know why the subpoenaing party might be seeking disclosure of private records and confidential information about a patient.

Arizona Divorce and Legal Separation

Arizona is a no-fault divorce jurisdiction. Either spouse may ask the court to dissolve the marriage for any reason or for no reason other than a desire to end the union. One of the parties must assert that the marriage is "irretrievably broken," but no other grounds for divorce from a non-covenant marriage are recognized in this state. A party's mental health may still be relevant to the divorce proceedings, however.

The only exception to Arizona's no-fault divorce is in the case of a **covenant marriage** which requires allegation and proof of more traditional, fault-based allegations to dissolve the marriage. A brief description of those statutory grounds elucidates what the client-spouse or adverse party-spouse may be attempting to prove with a mental health professional's subpoenaed records:

> The respondent spouse committed adultery; committed a felony crime and is in prison or is sentenced to death; abandoned the other spouse for at least a year; committed domestic violence or was physically, sexually, or emotionally abusive to someone in the household; or habitually abused drugs or alcohol. Separation is another ground for divorce, in that the spouses have been separated for two years; or a decree of legal separation was entered and the parties have since lived separate and apart for at least one year. Lastly, dissolution of a covenant marriage is possible

if the spouses both agree to a divorce. (See ARS § 25-903 for statutory language.)

Any of the circumstances relating to these grounds, or aspects thereof, may have been discussed in a confidential counseling session.

Arizona Child Custody and Parenting Time

In any child custody case, both parents are placed under rigorous examination for the purpose of determining what is in the children's best interests. Of course, both parties have an agenda and, with the help of legal counsel, a strategy to make that agenda come to fruition. When custody is contested, the pressure to identify one parent as better suited to take on the role of decision-making custody intensifies. Any meaningful information, including mental health records, regarding the parents' caretaking and child-rearing abilities may be crucial to the outcome of the custody case.

Making mental health information-gathering an objective of both parties, Arizona law requires that the judge consider all relevant factors pertaining to the child's "physical and emotional well-being" when making a custody decision in that child's best interests. ARS § 25-403.

A parent's mental disability is not presumed to be sufficient cause to deny custody or parenting time in Arizona, but it is one of many important factors for the court to consider. Quite simply, mental health records are often sought to prove a parent's strengths and weaknesses in a comparative fitness analysis. Ordinarily, however, a parent's request for child custody will not, in and of itself, act as an automatic waiver of his or her psychologist-client privilege, nor do mere allegations of mental instability or abuse from the other party.

Furthermore, a minor's mental health records may also be pertinent to what is in the best interests of the child-patient and that of other minors in the household. As with an adult, a child's confidential communications with the psychiatrist are privileged.

A few points about the minor's privilege are worth noting here. First, contrary to popular belief, parents are not always free to waive the privilege for their child. This issue of parental waiver is not specifically addressed in Arizona law.

Second, to speak for the child and to assert the minor's claim of privilege, the judge may appoint a **Best Interests Attorney** to represent the child's best interests; a **Child's Attorney** to represent the minor-client, being reasonably bound by the minor-client's directives and objectives; or appoint a **Court Appointed Advisor** to advise the court. ARFLP Rule

10. The judge's appointment of an attorney for the child is particularly likely when no parent is available to waive the privilege or when the parents' interests conflict with those of their child.

Third, when the child's safety is at issue, the psychotherapist or counselor has a duty to warn. In that instance, other ethical concerns would not apply as the judge will rule 100% on disclosing confidential mental health information to ensure the child's safety. And fourth, be prepared for varying opinions about these issues with judges interpreting the laws differently, depending upon the circumstances and jurisdiction.

Arizona Child Support

Child support orders go hand-in-hand with child custody determinations. ARS § 25-501. In any family law case involving minor children, a parent may claim that working outside the home is impracticable or impossible because of a child's mental health. If successful, such a position can affect the parent's obligation to pay child support and, quite possibly, shift more, most, or all of the financial responsibility on to the obligor-parent.

Arizona Spousal Maintenance

There is only one form of financial support in Arizona that may be awarded to a spouse or former spouse – that is, spousal maintenance. (Spousal maintenance takes the place of alimony.) A spouse's mental health may be a factor for the court to consider with any award of spousal maintenance to the man or the woman. ARS § 25-319(B)(3). Although the need for spousal maintenance is determined on a case-by-case basis, Arizona judges have broad discretion in awarding spousal support for any of the following reasons:

1. Spousal maintenance may be awarded to provide for the "reasonable needs" of a less-propertied, economically disadvantaged spouse. For example, an award could be appropriate in a marriage of long duration when the spouse is unable to achieve, with reasonable effort, an earning capacity that provides a standard of living after the divorce that is comparable to the standard of living enjoyed during the marriage. (Or, perhaps, to at least match the anticipated post-divorce standard of living available to the other spouse.)

2. Spousal maintenance may be awarded to provide for the spouse who is unable to achieve self-sufficiency through "appropriate employment." The recipient-spouse's mental health, for instance, could be shown to limit employment opportunities, living arrangements, or ability to live independently.

3. Spousal maintenance may be awarded to provide for the spouse who serves as "custodian of a child," when working outside the home is not feasible given the child's age or condition. The mental health of the custodian or the child could be relevant to an award of spousal support in this situation.

4. Spousal maintenance may be awarded to contribute to the economically disadvantaged spouse's educational opportunities. Awarded, for example, to assist the recipient-spouse in obtaining additional education, job skills, or training as a way of becoming "self-sufficient" following divorce – whatever is reasonably necessary to rehabilitate that spouse with the ultimate objective of financial independence. Establishing the recipient-spouse's psychological condition

and mental health needs plays strongly into the specifics of re-training and rehabilitating to achieve a greater level of financial independence following divorce.

5. Spousal maintenance may be awarded after a lengthy marriage, to provide for the mature spouse who is unlikely to find employment that pays enough to live independently. Age-related physical and mental health concerns and conditions may be important factors for the court to consider.

Although not spousal maintenance, an **equalization payment** may be part of the parties' property division in a divorce. And that one spouse may have a greater need for liquidity could influence the court's decision on who gets certain assets. For example, the judge may deem it proper to grant the spouse with mental health concerns or vulnerabilities additional cash while granting the other spouse more of the tangible property (house, vehicle, artwork, collections, and the like), or vice versa, depending upon the circumstances. The property division may be equal in value, but one spouse may have the greater liquidity – that is, he or she may walk away from the divorce with more cash.

4

APA Ethics Code: Conflicts with Law

Mental health professionals provide either psychotherapy or counseling, owing their primary duty to the patient. The American Psychological Association's **Ethical Principles of Psychologists and Code of Conduct** ("Ethics Code") lists five aspirational goals, one of which is to "respect the ... rights of individuals to privacy, confidentiality, and self-determination." The APA standards of conduct are enforceable rules and non-aspirational. All licensed mental health professionals must be intimately familiar with their applicable professional standards and ethics.

APA Standard 1 focuses on conflicts of law and professional ethics. When the practitioner is torn between upholding his or her ethical obligation to the client (such as maintaining confidentiality) and complying with the law (such as a subpoena), Standard 1.02 is instructive:

> *If psychologists' ethical responsibilities conflict with law, regulations or other governing legal authority, psychologists clarify the nature of the conflict, make known their commitment to the Ethics Code and* ***take reasonable steps to resolve the conflict*** *consistent with the General Principles and Ethical Standards of the Ethics Code. Under no circumstances may this standard be used to justify or defend violating human rights. [Emphasis added.]*

What is considered to be "reasonable steps" will depend upon the specific circumstances and the seriousness of the matter at hand.

Initially, hiring a licensed Arizona lawyer is always a reasonable first step when served with a subpoena for patient information. Objecting and filing a motion for protective orders may be the next reasonable step. Subpoena compliance without objection may be reasonable if the patient voluntarily signed a written release consenting to such disclosure. The circumstances, too, may dictate what is reasonable. The seriousness and potential consequences of a criminal child molestation case, for example, differ substantially from those raised in a civil divorce action.

[illegible]

5

How Subpoenas Differ from Court Orders

A subpoena is not the same as a court order. Therefore, responding to a subpoena differs from the duty to obey a court's order.

The subpoena is a writ to compel the mental health professional's testimony or production of things, issued by the Clerk of the Court when filed by the attorney as an officer of the court in a specific lawsuit. However, the judge is wholly responsible for issuing court orders. Court-ordered disclosure of patient information would follow a judicial hearing on what the practitioner must release. The judge decides what is and is not privileged, for example, or whether the scope of the subpoena is too broad (that is, a fishing expedition). An order from the judge takes precedence over other ethical responsibilities, arguably relieving the mental health professional from liability for testifying or making the ordered disclosures. In fact, violating a judge's order can result in contempt of court. Regarding the disclosure of confidential information without client consent, APA Standard 4.05(b) clarifies the practitioner's responsibility:

> *(b) Psychologists disclose confidential information without the consent of the individual only as mandated by law, or where permitted by law for a valid purpose such as to (1) provide needed professional services; (2) obtain appropriate professional consultations; (3) protect the client/patient, psychologist, or others from harm; or (4) obtain payment for services from a client/patient, in which instance disclosure is limited to the minimum that is necessary to achieve the purpose.*

Subpoenas and Court Orders Under HIPAA

Although too soon to know with certainty how the Patient *Protection and Affordable Care Act of 2010* will apply, do consider how subpoenas and court orders are handled under the *Health Insurance Portability and Accountability Act of 1996.* HIPAA protects patient information relating to the "past, present, or future physical or mental health or condition of an individual" in Arizona court proceedings and elsewhere.

Distinguishing between obeying a court order and complying with a subpoena under HIPAA, the U.S. Dept. of Health & Human Services advises that a health care provider "may disclose protected health information required by a court order," but before complying with a subpoena the health care provider must do more.

Specifically, he or she must determine whether the notification requirements of HIPAA's privacy rule are met. The provider should not respond to the subpoena without first obtaining some evidence that reasonable efforts were made to either: notify the person who is the subject of the information about the request, so the person has a chance to object to the disclosure, or to seek a qualified protective order for the information from the court. (See 45 CFR § 164.512(e).)

APA Standard 1.02 makes clear that reasonable steps should be taken whenever the practitioner's ethical responsibility conflicts with a subpoena for HIPAA-protected patient information. But deciding how best to proceed will depend upon the circumstances, the scope of the subpoena, and HIPPA law. It may be that the legal opinion of a HIPAA lawyer is also necessary, something the mental health professional's attorney will determine before moving ahead with an objection or motion for protective order.

Never Ignore a Subpoena

Certainly, a valid subpoena is a directive that cannot be ignored – it compels a response of some kind from the mental health professional. Importantly, the subpoenaed person's response is not necessarily what the subpoena directs. Just because the issuing attorney seeks broad release of patient information does not mean the psychotherapist or counselor must fully comply with the subpoena.

That is the most difficult situation for mental health professionals: determining appropriate compliance, if any, given professional ethical responsibilities under the APA's Ethics Code and those laws protecting patient privacy and privileged communications. Any response to a subpoena, then, should be approached with caution and possibly be limited in scope.

6
Types of Subpoenas

The requirements for a subpoena in family law cases are spelled out in the Arizona Rules of Family Law Procedure (ARFLP), Rule 52 – Subpoena. (See also Arizona Rules of Civil Procedure (ARCP), Rule 45.) As with the majority of states, Arizona recognizes two different forms of the subpoena.

First, the **subpoena ad testificandum** requires the subpoenaed person to appear and testify, typically at a deposition. But this would also include a subpoena requiring attendance at a hearing or trial. This subpoena may be served anywhere in Arizona, regardless of where the proceeding is to be held.

Second, the **subpoena duces tecum** requires the subpoenaed person to appear and bring the documents, records, or papers along, too. The psychotherapist or counselor may be ordered "to produce and permit inspection and copying of designated books, papers, documents, electronically stored information, or tangible things, or inspection of premises ..." ARFLP Rule 52(A)(1).

Arizona's family law rules of procedure also specify how the subpoena may be served on the mental health professional – that is, by someone authorized to serve process. Although any adult who is not a party to the lawsuit could personally deliver the subpoena, the practitioner is more likely to be served by a private process server or Arizona sheriff's deputy. Service is usually not by regular mail.

7

Special Concerns with Subpoenas for Raw Test Data

Of special concern is a request for raw psychological test data, whether the source of the request comes from the patient's own attorney or from the other party in a divorce, child custody dispute, or related family law case. There are pitfalls to avoid, ones unique to test data. There are also differences of opinion. Courts have ruled differently on this issue.

APA Ethical Duties Over Raw Test Data

There are many considerations raised by the Ethics Code regarding the release of raw test data. According to APA Standard 9.04:

> *(a) The term test data refers to raw and scaled scores, client/patient responses to test questions or stimuli and psychologists' notes and recordings concerning client/patient statements and behavior during an examination. Those portions of test materials that include client/patient responses are included in the definition of test data. Pursuant to a client/patient release, psychologists provide test data to the client/patient or other persons identified in the release.* ***Psychologists may refrain from releasing test data to protect a client/patient or others from substantial harm or misuse or misrepresentation of the data or the test****, recognizing that in many instances release of confidential information under these circumstances is regulated by law. [Emphasis added.]*

Without a patient's release, the practitioner is to "provide test data only as required by law or court order." APA Standard 9.04(b).

When ordered by the court to release raw test data, the mental health professional must comply with that order. But in the absence of a court order, the waters become murky. In particular, if test data will be misused or misinterpreted, then it may be withheld.

Interpretation of Raw Test Data By a Qualified Professional

When subpoenaed for the release of test data it is important to establish who will be responsible for interpreting those materials. Only offer to provide raw test data or materials to another mental health professional, someone who is qualified to interpret the data. Lay persons are not qualified to interpret raw test data. APA Standard 9.07, Assessment by Unqualified Persons.

Even when test data is turned over to a qualified individual, subsequent interpretations and professional opinions often differ. (For purposes of this discussion, assume that there is not a courtroom showdown between lawyers with two competing forensic psychologists.) The testing-process factors in many variables, including the "test-taking abilities and other characteristics of the person being assessed." APA Standard 9.06, Interpreting Assessment Results. When a qualified professional has reviewed the raw test data, she makes a determination based upon her own professional judgment, having never been the patient's therapist.

Owners of Test Materials, Kits, and Assessment Techniques

Publishers of test materials, kits, and assessment techniques that automate interpretations of patient data, for example, may expressly limit use of those tests to qualified mental health professionals only. Furthermore, there can be significant intellectual property concerns regarding the release of tests, mainly protection of copyrights and patented processes.

It may be possible, though, to protect the test's licensed-owner's intellectual property rights within the motion for protective order. Each licensed owner should have guidance regarding what to seek to protect with a motion for protective orders, including policies. Psychotherapists and counselors should check the testing service's website or call for technical assistance. The licensed owner may even provide very simple sample language for the protective order. In practice, test material that the licensed owner wants protected may not even be needed by the attorney issuing the subpoena.

may not even be needed by the attorney issuing the subpoena.

8

Complicating Matters with Inadequate Notice

There is always the possibility that the subpoena will not give the mental health professional sufficient time to reasonably respond, comply, or consult with an attorney regarding the scope of disclosure required by law. There is a question, then, whether the subpoena provides adequate notice.

Adequate Notice in a Subpoena

In general, the minimum time frame for compliance is about 15 days (although not affirmatively stated specifically under ARFLP Rule 52). Under ARS § 12-2294.01(A) regarding release of medical records, the "health care provider" must be served with the subpoena at least 10 days before the date for production.

The subpoenaed mental health professional has 14 days after being served (or within the time specified in the subpoena if earlier) to object, to seek a protective order, or to file a motion to quash or modify the subpoena. In the absence of an exception or waiver, "disclosure of privileged or other protected matter" is a reason to quash or modify a subpoena. ARFLP Rule 52. In some instances, the subpoenaed medical records could be delivered to the court under seal, but it is strongly recommended that the practitioner consult with an attorney before doing so. ARS § 12-2294.01(C-D).

If the psychotherapist or counselor encounters a scheduling conflict, is concerned with the adequacy of notice in the subpoena, or questions the subpoena's validity, those issues should be directed to an experienced Arizona attorney who represents the mental health professional only. *Never rely on a party's lawyer because of the potential for conflict of interest!*

When a subpoena is invalid for some technical reason, in most situations the practitioner should not gamble by failing to respond. Judges have the authority to sanction subpoena recipients who fail to comply. ARFLP Rule 52(E).

Extension of Time for Cause

Unless there is an emergency or pending hearing, if the records are voluminous, then the psychologist or counselor may request a reasonable extension of time to comply. That length of time may be negotiated and will depend upon the circumstances of the case and the quantity of documents to be produced.

In practice, many lawyers are less concerned about extending the time for production. They know from experience that judges will usually side with mental health professionals. An extension for cause will almost always be granted unless there is a hearing pending. However, if the records amount to a few pages or only minimal testing, and the psychotherapist or counselor launches no objections, then the extension need not be longer than a week or two ordinarily.

When a subpoena is invalid for some technical reason, in most situations the practitioner should not gamble by failing to respond. Judges have the authority to sanction subpoena recipients who fail to comply. (ARCP Rule 45(f)).

Extension of Time for Cause

Unless there is an emergency or pending hearing, [illegible]

[illegible]

9

Privileged Confidential Communications

Confidential communications between patients and their mental health professionals – physicians, psychiatrists, psychologists, licensed clinical social workers – are protected from disclosure absent a waiver from the patient. *Jaffee v. Redmond, 518 U.S. 1 (1996)*. It is the patient who holds the privilege, not the psychotherapist or counselor.

Arizona Mental Healthcare Privileges

More specifically, Arizona recognizes the following mental healthcare privileges:

- Doctor and patient privilege (ARS §12-2235);
- Priest or clergyman and penitent privilege (ARS §12-2233);
- Psychologist and client privilege (scope parallels attorney-client privilege) (ARS § 32-2085);
- Mediator and participant privilege (ARS § 12-2238);
- Domestic violence victim advocate and victim privilege (ARS § 12-2239); and
- Behavioral health professional and client privilege (scope parallels attorney-client privilege)(ARS § 32-3283).

Understand that the scope of protected communications allowed under each statutory privilege may vary significantly under Arizona law.

Patient's Waiver of Privilege

If the adult-patient waives the privilege and signs a release, then the practitioner is relieved of the duty to hold the confidence. A waiver may be express, implied, or automatic as when a patient puts his or her mental health at issue in a court case. *Bain v. Superior Court, 148 Ariz. 331, 334, 714 P.2d 824, 827 (1986).* With a child-patient, a parent or guardian ad litem could waive the privilege on behalf of the child. The APA Ethics Code allows the mental health professional to disclose confidential information with "appropriate consent" from the patient or from someone "legally authorized" to give consent on behalf of the patient, such as a guardian ad litem. Otherwise, disclosure of confidential information without consent is only permitted "as mandated by law" or to protect another from harm. APA Standard 4.05. (See Arizona's child abuse or neglect exception to privilege, ARS § 13-3620 and *Udall v. Superior Ct., 183 Ariz. 462, 904 P.2d 1286 (Ariz. App. 1995).*)

In an Arizona divorce with no minor children, clearly the court does not consider disclosure under the compelling "best interests" standard for custody purposes. Over issues of spousal maintenance and the division of assets and debts, a judge may be less inclined to order the release of confidential mental health records pursuant to subpoena. Required disclosure is less likely, especially when the patient-party did not waive the privilege in writing, did not consent to disclosure, and did not place his mental health at issue in the divorce. *Styers v. Superior Ct., 161 Ariz. 477, 478-79, 779 P2d 352 (Ariz. App. 1989).*

In the absence of a patient's waiver of the privilege, things can get rather dicey. With all family law cases, seek independent legal advice before disclosing fact-specific information, records, tests, or documents. With a child-patient, do not rely on legal advice from the parents' attorneys, instead seek independent legal advice. Always request a court order before testifying or disclosing privileged information. When in doubt, seek independent legal advice.

10

Challenging Subpoenas in Court

Looking again at ARFLP Rule 52 and the duty to respond and comply with a subpoena, the same rule also provides an exception. The psychotherapist or counselor may withhold information that is privileged. Objecting to the release of privileged patient information by filing a motion for protective orders puts the matter squarely before the judge to decide. The court may order the practitioner to comply with the subpoena, may modify the subpoena if unreasonable or oppressive, or may quash the subpoena altogether. Refusing to respond at all to a subpoena or objecting informally without filing a motion, however, may result in contempt of court.

When court-ordered, the mental health professional's release of confidential information without the patient's consent arguably does not violate the Ethics Code because said release was "mandated by law." APA Standard 4.05(b). To ensure that a court order is forthcoming, the practitioner may need to hire legal counsel to motion for protective orders. The judge will then rule on that motion. Should the judge order release of the mental health records, tests, or testimony, then the practitioner must comply with that order.

Leading Arizona cases indicate that the mental health professional who refuses to testify, after being ordered by the court to do so, will likely be held in contempt. However, the practitioner who testifies pursuant to the court's order can be immune from a lawsuit brought by the patient for breach of the duty of confidentiality.

Arizona's Mediation Privilege

In general, the presence of a third party waives the privilege that exists between doctor and patient. If someone else is in the room, ordinarily the privilege is waived (although that is less likely to occur practicably in domestic relations cases because we are dealing with families). An exception to that waiver is found in

Arizona's mediation privilege. ARS § 12-2238.

Mediation is confidential and nondiscoverable. That includes joint sessions where both spouses or both parents are with the mediator. Therefore, mediation records and notes are confidential and privileged for both spouses or parents. (Do be aware that judges have, on occasion, ruled to the contrary.) The public policy reasons behind this exception to third-party waiver is to protect marriages; and to encourage parents to participate in mediation when they need help resolving child custody disputes over parenting time, legal decision-making, supplemental child support, and permanent parenting plans.

There are four narrow exceptions to nondisclosure under ARS § 12-2238(B). Confidential mediation communications may be disclosed if any one of the following is so:

1. *All of the parties to the mediation agree to the disclosure.*
2. *The communication, material or act is relevant to a claim or defense made by a party to the mediation against the mediator ... arising out of a breach of a legal obligation owed by the mediator to the party.*
3. *The disclosure is required by statute.*

4. *The disclosure is necessary to enforce an agreement to mediate.*

Additionally, any threats or acts of violence occurring during mediation fall outside the protective umbrella of privileged communications and, therefore, may be disclosed by the mediator. Violence and threatened violence are, by definition, not privileged communication.

Arizona Cases on Waiver of the Psychologist-Patient Privilege

Bain v. Superior Court
148 Ariz. 331, 714 P.2d 824 (1986)

In a leading case on express and implied waiver of the psychologist-patient privilege under ARS § 32-2085, the Supreme Court of Arizona held in favor of the patient who filed a special action challenging the trial court's disclosure order of her marital counseling records.

The special action arose out of a medical malpractice lawsuit filed by Ms. Bain and her husband against Dr. Mills, the defendant surgeon, for having performed unnecessary surgery on her back.

In 1980, Ms. Bain entered into counseling with a psychologist, Dr. Lanyon. There were written tests, but only four sessions, all of which were "in connection with marital difficulties." These mental health records were at the heart of the special action before the Arizona Supreme Court.

In 1982, Ms. Bain fell from a ladder injuring her lower back. Pain persisted. Referred to the SW Regional Back Program at Good Samaritan Medical Center, Ms. Bain was psychologically evaluated and diagnosed with *conversion reaction* as the cause of her pain ("emotional stress being converted into physical symptomatology"). Her pain was "attributable to psychological factors that could not be relieved by surgery." Thereafter, Ms. Bain sought treatment from Dr. Mills.

Based solely upon his own testing and examination, Dr. Mills performed back surgery on Ms. Bain. He did not seek the patient's mental health records from Good Samaritan regarding her diagnosis prior to the surgery. The surgery did not improve her condition. Ms. Bain later underwent another operation with a different surgeon which resulted in neurological damage and permanent disability. She and her husband sued Dr. Mills for professional negligence and unnecessary surgery.

During pre-trial discovery, Ms. Bain was deposed and testified as to her counseling sessions with Dr. Lanyon. The defendant then sought production of mental health records from Dr. Lanyon. Ms. Bain filed a timely objection claiming the psychologist-patient privilege. After a hearing, the trial court ordered Dr. Lanyon to produce the mental health records. Objecting to the court's order and maintaining her right to protect confidential communications with a past treating-psychologist, Ms. Bain petitioned the Supreme Court. Ultimately, the Supreme Court agreed with Ms. Bain, holding that she had not waived the privilege, and remanded the case accordingly.

The Arizona Supreme Court's opinion provides a rule as to proper waiver of the psychologist-patient privilege:

> *[W]e hold that where a client waives the psychologist-patient privilege in writing or in court testimony, pursuant to § 32-2085, or pursues a course of conduct inconsistent with observance of the privilege, he has consented to disclosure of the information and has thereby waived the psychologist-patient privilege as to the confidential communication.*

Here are a few guidelines for practitioners following *Bain v. Superior Court*:

- Once the privilege attaches, testimonial disclosure is prohibited.
- The privilege attaches during pretrial

discovery and in court.

- Conduct constituting a waiver must be in writing or in court testimony.
- Conduct must indicate a "plain intention to abandon the privilege" to waive it. (Citing *Throop v. F.E. Young & Co., 94 Ariz. 146, 382 P.2d 560 (1963).*)
- Conduct constituting implied waiver includes the holder's offering herself as a witness and testifying voluntarily with regard to the privileged communication concerning the condition.
- The "scope of the implied [ARS § 32-2085] waiver ... only extends to privileged communications concerning the specific condition which has been voluntarily placed at issue by the privilege holder."
- The privilege holder's deposition testimony wherein she merely indentified the psychologist and the subject matter of the sessions is not sufficient, in and of itself, for implied waiver of the privilege. However, if the holder's deposition testimony went to "the substance of communications" with the psychotherapist, then that may be

an implied waiver.

- Only the holder of the privilege, and not her spouse, can waive it as to the patient's confidential communications with her psychologist.

The psychologist-patient privilege parallels the attorney-client privilege in scope, as does the doctor-patient privilege. That is not to say that the scope of all privileges is the same under Arizona law, however, for they may not be.

Lastly, you may be wondering who pays for the cost of dealing with a subpoena. The practitioner may have a claim for expenses, but more often than not the expense involved in production is borne by the psychotherapist or counselor. Should the practitioner provide professional time in dealing with the subpoena, then expert witness fees may be applicable. If compensable time, then it is the duty of the subpoenaing party to pay the practitioner for his or her professional time. Often, the claim for expenses should be negotiated by the mental health professional (or his or her legal counsel) in advance. In most situations, if requested in advance, a reasonable fee will be paid. If in dispute and a motion for protective order is filed, that issue should be brought before the judge and decided in court.

Styers v. Superior Court
161 Ariz. 477, 779 P.2d 352 (Ariz. App. 1989)

In this Arizona divorce, the husband filed a special action to prohibit his wife's discovery of his pre-marriage mental health records. As in *Bain*, he claimed the psychologist-patient privilege under ARS § 32-2085. The Court of Appeals agreed with husband, reversing the trial court's disclosure order.

At trial, the parties' dispute was over the division of community debts for which both spouses are responsible. The couple was married only six months, yet during that time husband incurred about $20,000 in psychiatric treatment debts. Wife sought to shift the entire treatment debt to husband on the theory that he did not tell her of his mental health history before they married. To bolster her case, she sought production of his pre-marital records from the Mohave County Mental Health Center.

Husband asserted his privilege and filed a motion to quash the subpoena, along with a motion to prohibit admission of his pre-marital mental health records into evidence. The trial court denied both motions, which was followed by his petition for special action.

Citing *Bain*, the appellate court held that husband's voluntary disclosure of pre-marriage treatment did not act as a waiver of the ARS § 32-2085 privilege, stating that "[o]ne may acknowledge the fact of treatment without consenting to the disclosure of its confidential details." Furthermore, the husband did not implicitly waive the privilege – he did not place his prior treatment at issue in the divorce. That is, merely seeking the equitable division of community property (and debts) in a dissolution proceeding does not put a spouse's pre-marital mental health condition at issue.

Emphasizing the need to avoid over-broad subpoenas for confidential mental health records, the court noted that:

> *Under wife's theory, the fact of her husband's prior treatment, its duration, and the diagnosis might be relevant to demonstrate that his current expenses arose from the treatment of the same condition.* ***This information, however, could have been sought by narrow, pointed discovery without wholesale invasion of the husband's confidential records.*** *[Emphasis added.]*

The Court of Appeals vacated the trial court's denial of husband's motion to quash the subpoena duces tecum, and remanded the case for proceedings consistent with the holding.

11

Conclusion

In conclusion, begin taking reasonable steps by hiring a licensed Arizona attorney to decide how best to approach dealing with the subpoena. A hearing may be requested to clarify what is sought in the subpoena, to challenge its validity, or seek to limit production.

The judge may require the production of documents *under seal* so that confidential information remains off the record. The judge may review the information *in camera* (privately in chambers). Testimony at a hearing may be taken to present concerns with sensitive information and the mental health professional's ethical duties to the patient.

The judge may clarify the subpoena's scope, may have the issuing attorney clarify, may modify the subpoena, may issue protective orders, or may quash the subpoena. Once the judge issues an order to disclose privileged information without a patient's consent, complying with that order avoids contempt and almost always protects the mental health professional should an action be brought later by that patient for breach of the duty of confidentiality.

About Scott David Stewart, Esq.

Born and raised in Phoenix, author Scott David Stewart, Esq., is the founder of the Stewart Law Group. With a select legal team, Mr. Stewart's vision was to establish a unique law firm singularly focused on the clients' experiences when dealing with difficult and often intensely emotional legal matters. Stewart Law Group represents clients in all matters of divorce, child custody, and family law.

Early in his career, Mr. Stewart was a Deputy County Attorney in the Major Crimes Division of the Maricopa County Attorney's Office. While there, Mr. Stewart honed his trial skills and developed the strategies for success that he continuously implements in all aspects of his law practice today. Since its formation, Stewart Law Group has earned the trust and respect of clients from all walks of life.

Mr. Stewart is a member of the State Bar of Arizona, Maricopa County Bar Association, and American Bar Association. He has an AV Preeminent® attorney-rating from Martindale-Hubbell® and is also rated "Superb" by Avvo, Inc. With more than 65 years of combined legal experience, Mr. Stewart and the attorneys with the Stewart Law Group are prepared to take on the most complex and challenging cases.

About Robert C. Howard, Jr., Esq.

Robert C. Howard, Jr., is an experienced family lawyer with the Stewart Law Group. He has practiced divorce and family law in Arizona since his admission in 1976 to the State Bar of Arizona and U.S. District Court, District of Arizona. Mr. Howard served as president of the Scottsdale Bar Association from 1985-1986 from which he received the Award of Excellence for Community Service (2006). He was in Class I of Scottsdale Leadership, served as its president from 1992-1993, and was honored with its Frank W. Hodges Alumni Achievement Award (1999) for excellence in community leadership. In 2011, Mr. Howard was inducted into the Scottsdale Historymakers Hall of Fame by the Scottsdale Chamber of Commerce.

Well known for his volunteerism and pro bono advocacy, Mr. Howard received the Maricopa County Bar association's Volunteer of the Year Award (2000) and Longevity Award for Outstanding Performance in the Family Lawyers Assistance Project (2014). The Arizona bar named him among the Top 50 Pro Bono Attorneys in 2008.

Mr. Howard's family moved from Brooklyn, New York, to Arizona in 1960. He graduated from ASU with a Bachelor's Degree in Political Science and a Juris Doctorate from ASU Law School where he was on the law review. In addition to his family law practice and divorce seminar presentations, Bob, as he is known by friends and clients alike, is also a stand-up comic and humor columnist.

Stewart Law Group

777 E Thomas Rd Ste 210, Phoenix AZ 85014
Phone: 602.548.4600

1490 S Price Rd Ste 212, Chandler AZ 85286
17470 N Pacesetter Way, Scottsdale AZ 85255
14050 N 83rd Ave Ste 290, Peoria AZ 85381
1910 S Stapley Dr Ste 221, Mesa AZ 85204
20325 N 51st Ave Ste 134, Glendale AZ 85308

www.ArizonaLawGroup.com

Made in the USA
Monee, IL
04 November 2026

67378656R00046